If You Would Love Me

10 August 2018

For Joel and Frances,

with love,

Patricia

poems by

Patricia Sheppard

Patricia Sheppard

Finishing Line Press
Georgetown, Kentucky

9 August 2016
For Rob and Frances
with love,

If You Would Love Me

in memoriam
Charles G. K. Warner
historian, *raconteur*, dear friend

Acknowledgments

Grateful acknowledgment is made to the editors of the following journals and publications in which these poems first appeared:

The Antioch Review: "After Sappho," "The Twin Pines"
The Hudson Review: "Advertisement," "The Whistling Swans"
Intro 8: "*Nu Descendant un Escalier*," George Garrett, editor (Doubleday)

Publisher: Leah Maines
Editor: Christen Kincaid
Cover Photograph: "Granite Woman I," by Karin Rosenthal
Author Photograph: Darren Pellegrino
Cover Design: Lyn Markey

Printed in the USA on acid-free paper.
Order online: www.finishinglinepress.com
also available on amazon.com

Author inquiries and mail orders:
Finishing Line Press
P. O. Box 1626
Georgetown, Kentucky 40324
U. S. A.

Table of Contents

Advertisement

If you would love me,
you must love abandon,
putting aside everything
the self has arranged around itself.

A snake beginning its moult,
not knowing why it should leave its skin
to go, as if for the first time
into the world, goes.

The soul can run free then,
while the body is reforming.
How happy the soul is.
I can promise you that much.

The Little Words

My kindergarten was *Mater Dolorosa*
down the block, but before that,
my mother was my school.

Newspaper on the floor, her pen circling
the little words for me
because, she said, I was little, too.

*There's an 'a.' This is an 'an' and
here's an 'and.' That: 'A, T,' … 'at.'*
'A, S,' … 'as.' Then, my turn

to find the little words: *of, by, up.*
Once I saw one, I saw them everywhere.
So, in, or.   *What's an 'of?'*

Afterwards, she held me.
I made my heart beat
with hers. I liked the smell of her skin.

Some days, though, she would cry all day.
When I brought my blanket to her,
she would push me away. I wanted

to be with her and all the little words we found
whose work it is
to demonstrate relationship.

How I Learned My Numbers

I saw her write with a yellow pencil
while talking on the telephone.
She went back to the kitchen.

I wanted to practice my numbers
all by myself.

She came back to the phone,
looked at the paper where I had traced
over her numbers and made a call.

I knew she'd be proud of me because
I was a big girl and could write my numbers,

but her face went all strange and her voice, too.
Come here. You made me dial a wrong number.
She hit me so hard I soared across the room.

I knew, then, that I could fly.

Girl Running Errand

Almost home, I heard a voice,
raw as a cut on jagged glass,
then, children crying.

I stopped exactly in the middle
of the live oak's shade.
I realized the shrieking

was my mother's, the children,
my sisters and brothers.
I wanted to keep walking

up the street, into another house
where a woman would kiss me
and let me be her daughter.

The milk was no longer cold
on my arm. I must have stood there
a long time, as the sun reddened

and sank, knowing, all the while,
that I would have to go back inside,
through that back kitchen door.

The Ring

She said it would be mine,
in time.
I begged it from her.
Shallow green stone, color of the Gulf
of Mexico at the shore, white gold
setting, filigree. It had been hers as a girl.

Day after day, I returned.
In the waves, I could hear us splashing
and through our laughter
tried to reconstruct
that sudden arc of loss
when the ring slipped from my finger.

Each day is different with the tide.
I would search the changes of the sun
through the emerald-bright water,
but always there was only
the washed green color of my ring
and the froth-foamed splashing.

Laundry Day At The YWCA

Stuff the bottom sheet in the pillowcase.
Take fresh ones from the stack.
Use your top sheet for the bottom.
Effective economy.

For seventy-five dollars a week,
I was safe, at least, for the time being.
If it's *fight or flight,*
I'd had enough of fighting.

Call me *a troubled girl,* if you like,
but I was running away from trouble,
as fast as I could, with one clean sheet
between me and the rest of the world.

Fledgling

I took my leave of Florida,
bird of passage, who flew
north for the winter.

The snow's blank fields
are a far cry from the dunes,
the sand holding heat.

Florida was never frugal. She
was casual with her flowers,
careless in her attractions.

I shall not return, even though
there are no orange trees
on Orange Street and I am afraid.

The Hot House Plant

These tropical orange blossoms
are making me delirious
this Connecticut evening.
They make a young girl want to marry.

Alas, I am married.

The wedding flowers are weeping.
The night is moist. I am not
in love with you.
I wish I could offer us a balm

for the sadness diffused
in this scented and disappointed air.

Nu Descendant un Escalier

It is the inside of the year.
Snow is on the river.

I find myself
on the staircase
holding only color
in my wake.
I move when I stand still.

Was I going upstairs,
tired, to bed?
Or, did I sleep well,
and with whom, and
start down for bread and cheese?
I now face
what I believe to be east.

So this is the beginning,
standing naked on the stairs.

At Delphi

Far from marbled Athens, I went,
a slow pilgrimage
under the unrelenting Grecian sun.
All the long climb up,
the rocks loose in the thirsty sand,
I felt I would fall,
another rock on the rocks below.

Wild poppies sparsely grew,
the last blood of Delphi
not drained away.
I gathered them as I walked.

Each flower added to my skirt
quickened the terror in my blood.
Flowers for those I lost, dark flowers
of failure. Red flower of survival,
crimson guilt. Flower of grief,
quarreling with other sorrows,
heaped as a pattern along the mind.

All bled together
in the gauze basin of my skirt.
I dropped the poppies on Apollo's altar
and watched them wither on the stone.

Happy are they who enter my house
and cast no shadow.

Persephone

At first, I thought they must be rubies
they were so brilliant by the lantern
(and my husband is fond of jewels),
yet when I grew closer, I saw
on his table of dark-veined marble,
fruit my mother might have sent me
out to pick after dinner. How homesick
I felt then, missing the orchard.

Some say I was hungry after the long journey.
I had no appetite. He held me
down. The bitter, chambered,
faceted pomegranate
seed,
red,
bright
as my blood.

Something Startling, This Desire

The waves closed over Poseidon.
Not until the last century,
in a window of time
between the Great Wars,
did the sea surrender
The Poseidon of Artemision
from the fifth century,
before the common era.

He looks contemplatively at the ages
fixing them in his glance,
his arm raised to hurl his trident
into our lives,
striking open a spring,
something startling, this desire
for the *ideal* in us
that will not be drowned.

After Sappho

A pretty woman afraid
her lover might think her
ugly, should she allow
vehement Eros
to distort her face
with passion's blaze,
kept her modest beauty.

Oh, Aphrodite, show her
there is no shyness
between women.

Column And Oleander

The oleander grows
near the morning shade
of the Doric order.

It likes a ruined temple,
an ancient hillock to cling to,
the air, arid.

Come, enter the pronaos,
you are young. The sky is clear
and the sweet oleander, bright.

I am the hidden pin centering
the column drums.
I let the sharp sun's edge hang

inside the flutes, then slash
the emblematic days, one by one.
They die by fire always.

How lovely you are.
Time will take your beauty.
See the women wearing black?

Stone can bear all things,
though pock-marked
as the hoary moon,

the slow erosion of hope
and the poisonous oleander.

Santa Maria Della Salute

I went into the twilit rotunda
where the heavens are drawn to earth
in one translucent column,

the circumference of which
is so wide, were it a tree,
it would date to creation

and the naming of the first woman
for the intimate form of light:
Eve.

Muguets

You brought me
muguets,
the little lilies

of the valley
trucked in early
from Brittany,

pungent
out of proportion
to their size,

old fashioned,
a quiet glade caught
in a shaft of sun,

something
of the obsolete,
flowers,

the name for which
used to mean
a *beau*, as well,

shy
in their broad-leaved
bouquets;

where this leaf
was pulled
from the ground,

one white filament
trails,
determined to root

in my heart's
first sure sign
of spring.

25, Avenue Des Champs-Élysées

The Prince wore a canary yellow tie.
He sat next to the gold bathtub

in the Marquise de Païva's
(grandest of the Grand Horizontals)

bathroom where we were dining.
A toast, then, to the *ancien régime:*

On the Bourse today, in heavy trading,
gold closed slightly higher.

The Islands

We woke to the ocean,
not a conch
held to the ear,
but the real tide ebbing.
The mosquitoes all around
made a peaceful drone
heard at the lull
between the waves.
The netting, knotted
at the ceiling, overhead,
stirred around us,
showing us
the veiled prospect
of a bride trembling.

The Critic

The woman to the side in the plain cloth coat
is clenching her teeth; the women in ermine
are all smiles and diamonds in wartime,

swirling past her in velvet and lace, tickets
in hand, soft clutch, ephemera of orchids,
and, *God save the Queen,* those tiaras.

Weegee had the scowling lady show us
the opera goers were what was wrong
with America, and the Germans who,

loving opera possibly more than the two women,
took their picture for propaganda, printing it
on leaflets that would litter the beach-head,

their photograph placed just above
the one of the surf and the Marine
with the perfect bullet hole in his back:

YANK SOLDIER, WHILE YOU ARE DYING
ON ANZIO, AT HOME, THE OPENING OF THE
OPERA HAS NEVER BEEN MORE BRILLIANT.

The one to the left, the blonde, has a son,
a young Lieutenant, handsome devil.
He enlisted through the silk-stocking

regiment, the Old Seventh, was schooled
in the Knickerbocker Greys
where Major Smith, that old dandy,

drilled them up one side of the Park
Avenue Armory and down the other,
as he intoned, ***THE SPARTANS WERE*** ....

For their part, the choir boy voices,
yielding to the onslaught of testosterone,
cracked, in several registers, as they replied,
*the **brav**-est of men.*
WHAT MADE THEM BRAVE?
Dis-*ci-pline!*

He was under fire, at Anzio,
when he saw her half-buried in the sand,
her picture. *Maman!* and Lady Decies.

In the middle of a war, for God's sake.
Brava, Maman, a sense of irony, after all.
Never around much before and here you are.

That horrid French governess, who boxed my ears
until I got the pronunciation exactly, 'Non!
Non!' The maids, the butler, the other servants.

The dress suits—every day,
one must keep up appearances, after all.
My father, who left early on with a chorus girl,

off to Florida. The money all on mother's side,
mother's father, the Colonel, hated 'that SOB
she married, who had nothing, was nothing

but a drunk.' Between cigars,
he took every opportunity
to announce his prediction,

turning his head towards me,
'The apple doesn't fall far from the tree.'
The townhouse on East 62nd, just off 5th,

now, this foxhole. You had a flair for the dramatic,
Maman, all the fancy ball gowns, yet another
engagement, dashing to the doorway breathless;

I can almost read the stage direction—stopping,
'Ah! mon petit chou,' leaning down to kiss me
always on the top of my head.

Your diamonds were cold and hard,
Maman, hitting me in the face,
Maman, as you rushed out to the opera.

Fall Crocuses And Other Spring Flowers

Haven't you seen them? What? The violets,
the purple hearts marching out near Veterans' Day.
And the stray forsythia, the azalea, the quince
blossoms. Did you miss them? You did?
Have you been going to New York again?

I was thinking about you,
what to get for your birthday.
You're impossible! You have everything.
This year even the government chimes in.
Sixty-five. The Age of Social Security.

Mild, mid-November. It was exhilarating
raking leaves. I threw off my jacket.
I raked more leaves and more,
sent my sweater sailing, ran,
jumped in the leaves.

Then,
I saw them,
pale and elongated,
a row of crocuses straggling
over a bank of dry oak leaves.

You could say it was cruel
to be fooled out of season,
the temperature, the length of darkness,
simulating spring by coming from the equinox
part way from the other side.

No one would argue
these were the crisp flowers of *Primavera*.
They were lying on their sides, pulling
their bodies along, but, please,
they weren't duped. They knew.

Spring. That's easy. Sex,
immortality, we breathe it in
with the impossibly perfumed air
all through a night of love,
as though it would last forever.

Wasn't it yesterday you were a young man,
when you first saw the women of Europe,
when the boys killed in war
were not gone, but glorified,
kept in amber by classmates and widows?

How did you get so bald?
(Though there's a bit left
to comb.)
Why the thicker glasses
and the back side tooth missing?

You might say the fall crocuses were wounded. Yes,
they were tired as they rested there, but gaudy spring
never shaded lavender with white as subtly
as in their stretched striations. What they reach for,
they embrace: the last of the year's sun.

Brave messengers.
News of a second chance.

I Knew She Would Wait

I knew she would wait until today,
their Wedding Anniversary.
When I drove over early this morning

she was propped up in the landscape
outside the kitchen door
where the bridal wreath used to grow.

Her pink and white checked robe
clashed with the red brick house
she never liked (*his* parents' house).

My father was in her car on the lawn,
edging forward to the back porch
under the walnut tree.

A week ago, I found her on the floor
on all fours, growling at shadows.
Back in bed, her legs spread, knees up,

*Yes, I'm pushing. I **am** pushing.*
She came to. *What day is this?*
How many days till July 27th?

We got her in the car. He braked for a red light.
I said, *Run it*. He did and all the rest of them
to Sacred Heart. Rush of wheelchair, consent forms.

Her last signature was an up and down ziz-zag
stitch that looked something like the first letter
of *Mary* over and over again. I took away the pen.

She mumbled, now, in the cadence of ranting,
no words left. I pulled the window curtain open.
She kept trying to get up, pleading with her eyes.

I could read her.
If she could get out, it couldn't happen. She butted
her head towards the door, fought as I held her,

as I laid her head back, slowly, surely, on the pillows.
I saw a crazed animal cornered in her eyes.
Fear has a smell to it.

The night she took off in the station wagon
with one of the hunting rifles (kept in the space
between the china cabinet and the dining room wall,

even with seven kids in the house, loaded),
I followed her in the other car as she careened
through town and stopped, at last, out of gas,

still pushing the accelerator when I caught up.
She was going to kill us both. That night
I talked her down. The next morning,

not a word.
I knew she could hear me,
as I spoke to her, *Shush, shush, now,*

anything that came to mind, little cooing
sounds, singsong; I kept holding her hand,
stroking her arm, rhythmically, so her breathing

could follow and, finally, it did: steady
shallow, rapid, rattling. *I love you, Mama,*
caught in my throat, but I got it out, *I do*

love you, Mama. Her voice was almost drowned;
she was making gurgling sounds, her face puffed up,
as her liver gave out and the internal bleeding

took over, jaundice spreading to blue-purple.
Across her chest, the telltale red tracks
of spider angiomas. Her body kept bloating.

An orderly pushing a cart in the corridor stopped,
Was she in a car crash? She was
heartbreakingly beautiful when she married.

My sisters and brothers arrived with the priest.
From the host, he broke a tiny sliver,
put it in her mouth, Viaticum, the rest in his.

Hail Mary, full of grace, the Lord is with thee…
She was staring out the window, her eyes
part of the same blue sky she could still see.

My sister said, *You've been here since 6*
*and Daddy left? You need a break. **No**.*
It was my watch, my feet planted. **Go**.

Ten minutes later, I dropped the coffee
and bolted for the stairs.
She had been staring at something,

now at nothing. I felt the room list.
It's like that on a ship, one minute
you're level, the next, you're walking sideways.

Her look, that empty blue look I saw
had always been there, just underneath.
The doctor closed her eyes.

My father took off the wedding ring
he had put on her left ring finger
thirty-two years ago today,

the ring she, as a matter of sacrament,
had worn since then, explaining carefully
to the nurses before each delivery and to

the anesthesiologist before the hysterectomy
that they would have to tape her ring
because she would not take it off

and my father broke down. None of us,
ever, had seen him cry. We stood there.
The priest led us in prayer.

I was not there when she died. Then, I knew
that she would wait. She did not want to die
in front of me whose life she took

as reproach to hers—because I broke free,
her will propelling her to her Anniversary and
a little longer till I left. That was just like Mother.

The hush lifted, though no one spoke
above a whisper and not much, at that,
as we began to file out. A nurse pulled me aside.

She asked me to help undress her.
I looked at the wreck of her dead body,
her belly swollen full term,

the body that had quickened
and given birth to us.
Hers was a long, slow, foundering.

I wanted to throw myself on her,
cover her, keep her
warm, the cold settling, already,

irreparably, in.
I left with a wadded up
blue nylon nightgown.

My father wanted no autopsy
and the cause of death to read:
Cardiac Arrest.

The doctor allowed it, however,
she did not die of a heart attack,
although, yes, her heart stopped beating,

eventually, and, no, she did not die,
one more dead drunk,
in the gutter.

She died in the Southern manner,
the bourbon in the sideboard,
the silence all around her,

but it all comes to the same thing.
I have to tell someone,
I cannot not tell someone.

My Father's Penis

Uncut. I hadn't known that.
Crumpled, and, as he says,

It's not working anymore,
hence, the suprapubic catheter

I swab with alcohol at the site.
I clean him after a bowel movement,

apply lanolin to his bed sores,
get a diaper. My father has a few weeks left.

I am here to make him comfortable.
He was surprised—my appearance

by his side—as I have always been
one Athena of a headache for him.

On the facts of life, my mother,
tired of questions, sent me

to him, who had studied Anatomy
in Dental School.

About foreplay, I wouldn't know.
Certainly, my father's penis hardened

and thrust into my mother.
Of the millions of possibilities,

given his semen with her ovum,
I was the result.

I would like to think they had pleasure,
that I had been conceived in joy.

The Pines: A Triptych

I. The Grandmother Pine

The boughs are so high they are a mystery.
The tree sings as she sweeps
her stars from the infinite.

The tree shines. The very tips
of the pine, glazed by the sun,
are white with clarity,

the needles so distinct
they are transparent,
interchangeable with the sun.

And the pine brightens
if that is possible,
until the needles tremble.

Within the trunk's deep crevices,
inside her secretly ringèd heart,
she holds each moment,

the moment encircles the years
and an ancestral corridor adjoins the ages.

II. The Mother Pine

The dead pine leans on the living.
A tarnish of bark remains
in memoriam. The skeletal limbs
that once reached up and out, bow under,
tangling indistinctly with the next branch down.
The lower ones sag to the ground
in an attitude of supplication.
The dry needles hang and shiver,
not shimmer, in the wind.
Their metallic sound rings
against a world it was never fully part of,
a silvered voice blackened by fear.
The death she did not come back from
is the silver, not the golden, bough.

III. The Twin Pines

When two pines begin to grow together,
the one arcs its outer limbs
around itself in an aura
and speaks, under the aegis of the sky,
as if from an amphitheater,
to the other, who in turn,
has circled its shining limbs
halfway round to greet the other,
singing in a mellifluous voice,
under the milk-blue sky.
The trees embrace,
in the wind, they whisper,
the sound of silk on satin,
this reciprocity, this harmonious
strophe and anti-strophe.

Between the pines, the inner branches intertwine,
though the trunks on the near side are,
for the most part, stark.
The limbs are bare and dark,
the lower ones break and fall away,
as the old guardians of their solitudes die.
They face each other then,
each to the interior of the other,
their being joined.
Their voices rise in conversation,
tossing on the high, exquisite wind,
and the revelation is continuous
as the unfolding of time,
as time devolves upon them.
I praise the love between us.

The Whistling Swans

I have never heard a sound like that before,
the sound the air makes when it speaks,
as hollow as the bones of a bird,
as precisely fierce as the beak.
The feathers that lift the swans overhead
guide arrows to their destination,
thus, these sounds pierce the heart purely.

Notes

Nu Descendant un Escalier: The painting referenced is *Nu Descendant un Escalier* (No. 2), by Marcel Duchamp, 1912, Philadelphia Museum of Art, first exhibited in the United States in NY at The Armory Show, 1913.

The Critic: Photograph of same name by Weegee (Arthur Fellig), published in *LIFE Magazine*, December 6, 1943.

The Twin Pines: The phrase, "guardians of their solitudes," refers to and adapts a passage in Rilke's letter of Feb. 12, 1902 to Paula Modersohn-Becker, "...I hold this to be the highest task of a bond between two people: that each should stand guard over the solitude of the other." *Letters of Rainer Maria Rilke*, 1892-1910, Trans. by Greene & Norton, W.W. Norton & Co. (New York 1945).

Patricia Sheppard is a graduate of Yale College, the University of Iowa's Writers' Workshop and College of Law. She is a Visiting Scholar at Brandeis University's Women's Studies Research Center. Her poems have appeared in *The Antioch Review, The Hudson Review, The Iowa Review*, and elsewhere.